ALL THINGS KOALAS FOR KIDS

FILLED WITH PLENTY OF FACTS, PHOTOS, AND FUN TO LEARN ALL ABOUT KOALA BEARS

ANIMAL READS

WWW.ANIMALREADS.COM

THIS BOOK BELONGS TO...

_____

_____

WWW.ANIMALREADS.COM

CONTENTS

Welcome to the Cuddly World of Koalas!	1
What Is a Koala?	5
Are There Different Species of Koalas?	17
The History of Koalas	23
Unique Characteristics and Appearance of Koalas	33
The Life Cycle of Koalas	49
Bonus!	55
How to Help the Koalas from Afar!	61
Thank You!	67

WELCOME TO THE CUDDLY WORLD OF KOALAS!

Australia is famously home to some of the world's most unique animals. Among the many weird and wonderful creatures that call this amazing country home, koalas are undoubtedly the most adored.

These cuddly, huggable teddy bears are famous for being supremely slow, lovably lazy, and ridiculously cute. Yet behind the furry facade lies a unique and complex creature unlike any other.

*Are koalas **really** bears? Are they truly as placid and huggable as they look? Do they seriously survive only on eucalyptus, or are they, perhaps, widely misunderstood?*

Join us as we head *Down Under* and dive into the wondrous world of koalas. Using our **koalafications** as extreme animal lovers, we'll uncover all the fascinating mysteries about this iconic animal and learn its deepest secrets.

Ready to get to know the koala?

Let's go!

WHAT IS A KOALA?

Let's begin our journey by dispelling a most crucial myth: *koalas are **not** bears.* They are **arboreal marsupials**.

What does *arboreal* mean?

Arboreal comes from the ancient Latin word for tree (*arbor*) and denotes an animal that spends most of its life on trees. Aside from koalas, arboreal animals include monkeys, squirrels, parrots, and lizards, among many more. Some arboreal animals can fly, swim or walk and run on the ground, yet what they all have in common is that they spend *most* of their time on trees.

*What does **marsupial** mean?*

A marsupial is a very special kind of mammal. Marsupials give birth to undeveloped babies that crawl into their mum's pouch on instinct to complete their development. When marsupial babies are born, they are blind and unable to survive, yet their instincts drive them to hang on to their mom's fur and locate her pouch. This means a marsupial spends half of the pregnancy inside its mother's body and half outside!

The most famous marsupials are koalas, kangaroos, wallabies, wombats, and opossums. Australia is home to most of the world's marsupials, although a few species are also found in the Americas – most of them in South America. North America only has one marsupial animal: *the Virginia opossum.*

FUN FACT: When British explorers first landed in Australia in the late 1700s, they came across an animal they had never seen before: a greyish-colored bear-like creature with a pouch! They named it the 'koala bear' in English because they had never before encountered a marsupial and simply assumed it must have been a *type* of bear. Koala is what indigenous Australians called the animal. A word that is thought to mean 'no water' in various indigenous languages. Soon enough, biologists realized they had encountered a whole new creature altogether, yet the name '*koala bear*' stuck forever.

Koalas are **herbivores** *meaning they only eat plants.*

Wondering what the difference is between an herbivore and a vegetarian? A vegetarian is someone who chooses to not eat meat, and an herbivore is an animal not able to eat meat because its digestive system is not built for it. In short: a vegetarian chooses to eat only plants, whereas a herbivore must eat only plants!

Koalas are notorious for being totally obsessed with eucalyptus leaves. Most of their diet consists of this very fragrant plant, found all over Australia. Despite what many people think, however, koalas can eat other leaves as well, and we'll learn all about that in later chapters.

Koalas are **nocturnal** animals, which means *they are most active during the night.* One of the reasons koalas are thought of as sublimely lazy is because they are usually seen sleeping during the day. But this is what a nocturnal animal does! It sleeps all day long and is most active during the cooler nighttime hours. This is when a koala heads off in search of food. *Mind you, a koala can easily spend 18 hours a day sleeping, so in all honesty, they may just be as lazy as they seem!*

FUN FACT: Being a nocturnal animal is awesome for survival. It is much safer to look for food when predators can't see you well. Plus, it helps to be nocturnal in hot countries! Being nocturnal helps you avoid moving around (*and using more energy*) in the hottest hours of the day. Other examples of nocturnal animals are bats, owls, badgers, and foxes.

In the wild, koalas can live up to 18 years of age. A fully-grown adult is about 30 inches tall and weighs about 30 pounds. Koalas have a round body with a large head, round fluffy ears, and no tail. The most distinctive characteristic of a koala is its adorable, spoon-shaped nose. Fur colors range between brown and smokey gray.

A male koala is called a **buck**, while a female is a **doe**. Male koalas are usually larger than female ones. They also have larger and darker noses.

Baby koalas are called **joeys**, and you will surely agree that they are one of the cutest animals on earth.

Today, researchers estimate there are only 50,000 to 100,000 koalas left in the Australian wilderness. This slow and gentle creature is listed as **endangered** and is fervently protected in its homeland. Despite protection, however, koalas are often the most affected wildlife victims of bushfires.

Unlike kangaroos that can run away and wombats that can burrow underground, koalas have no escape route in case of a forest fire. Over the last 20 years, Australia's koala population has been decimated by natural disasters, habitat loss, and disease.

Luckily, a wave of koala protection initiatives is underway in Australia to help preserve and boost the country's koala population.

In Australia, you will find koalas living in the wild where their beloved eucalyptus forests are prevalent. This is most common in the eastern and southern regions of the country. If you wish to visit Australia to see koalas in the wild, you may want to pin the states of New South Wales, Victoria, Queensland, and South Australia on your travel map!

Australia is the only country in the world where koalas live in the wild. They are **endemic** to the country, which means they are natives of Australia and were not introduced by humans.

ARE THERE DIFFERENT SPECIES OF KOALAS?

Alas, there is only one koala species, although experts have identified three **subspecies** living in three distinct regions of Australia. To be honest, even this statement could cause a lot of arguments among experts. Some believe there are more than three subspecies, while others believe there are no subspecies at all.

FUN FACT: A species is any group of animals that can breed and make babies with one another. If a small group is separated from the main herd and spends a long time in a different location, however, it can develop unique traits that help it survive in this location. Say, like thicker fur because it is a colder environment. These are traits that other members of its species living elsewhere do not have. These traits now make it a distinctive subspecies.

Whatever the case may be, and whether or not true subspecies of koalas exist, it is certainly true that koalas can look different depending on where they live in Australia. Those living in the southern states tend to be larger than their northern siblings. They also have thicker, fluffier, and darker coats.

Why would a southern Australian koala develop such distinct characteristics, you may wonder?

Experts believe that it's all due to the climate. Australia may be known as a tropical country, but this is only true of the northern region. The southern regions, in reality, can experience quite cold winters. In Victoria, for example, temperatures can easily drop below freezing in winter! Scientists believe it's for this reason that southern koalas developed bigger bodies and thicker fur. These different traits help them cope with the winter cold!

Amazingly, the central Australian region of New South Wales (which lies in between the cooler and hotter regions) is home to yet another koala species that appears to be distinct. Koalas here have developed fascinating in-between characteristics. They are larger than northern koalas yet not quite as large as the southern ones, and they also have slightly thicker, furrier, and darker coats.

Isn't it cool to know that where a creature is born is directly responsible for how they look? How dark the skin or hair is, and even the size of its body?! The animal world is truly fascinating, and the koala world is even more so!

WHAT DO YOU CALL A LAZY KOALA?

A pouch potato!

THE HISTORY OF KOALAS

How did koalas end up in Australia, and why are they only found in the country? Are they related to any other living animal today?

It's time to travel back in history and discover where these most fascinating creatures originated.

Up until 45 million years ago, Australia was part of a much bigger continent known as Gondwana. This ancient continent was very big and comprised what we now know as Australia, New Zealand, Africa, Antarctica, and South America.

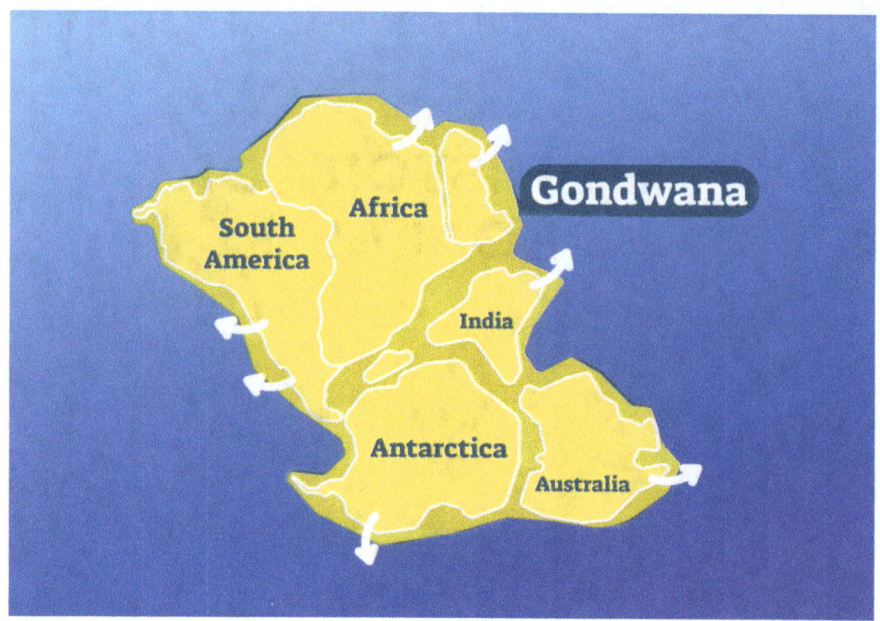

Scientists believe that koala-like animals already existed in the part of Gondwana that later became Australia long before the continent split apart. This is even though the oldest known **fossil** ever found of a koala ancestor dates back only 25 million years. Yes, we agree that is a *very* long time ago, but in fossil terms, it isn't.

FUN FACT: Fossils are remains of living creatures that are considered to be older than 10,000 years. The oldest fossil ever found on earth was discovered in Australia, and it was 4-billion-year-old bacteria!

Alright...where were we?

Ancient koalas!

As it turns out, the ancestors of the modern-day koalas were likewise terrible swimmers. Once Australia became a separate continent, and its geography changed, koalas (*and all other animals*) developed unique traits that helped them survive what is, essentially, a very harsh country. This is why Australia is home to so many animals, like koalas, kangaroos, and wombats, that are not found anywhere else on earth.

Experts do agree on one thing, however: the 'koala' population that was stuck on the Australian continent must have been the only one in existence on Gondwana at the time of the split. *How do they know?* Because there is no other animal in the world today that resembles or is related to the koala in *any* way. If there had been, we would have probably discovered it by now!

HUMAN INFLUENCE ON THE HISTORY OF THE KOALA IN AUSTRALIA

Australia had been inhabited by indigenous people for 60,000 years before the arrival of the British in 1788. The local indigenous population revered the koala and the animal featured in many of their legends. Although Australia's Aboriginal people hunted the koala for food, the animal thrived because the consumption was always kept at a minimum.

By the time Europeans arrived on the continent, an estimated 10 million koalas were thought to have been living in Australia's forests. Yet Europeans soon identified the koala as an excellent source of fur, and hunting of the animal, in great numbers, began almost immediately.

Within just 150 years of British arrival in Australia, koalas in South Australia, Victoria, and New South Wales, were hunted to near-extinction.

Finally, in the 1930s, the koala was recognized as a unique and irreplaceable wildlife species. Various laws were introduced to protect the animal, and although the koala population did recover somewhat, it still needs a lot of protection today. Koalas may no longer be hunted for their fur in Australia. Yet, their beloved trees are still cut down regularly and in large quantities. So koalas are now in great danger of **extinction** due to habitat loss.

DO KOALAS HAVE ANY LIVING RELATIVES TODAY?

The koala's closest living relative is another Australian icon: *the super-sweet* **wombat**! Wombats are land-dwelling marsupials that grow as large as a medium-sized dog. They have short legs, a round and stocky body, and an adorably chubby face. If you were to see a close-up photo of a koala and a wombat's face, you could definitely see the family resemblance!

Much like koalas, wombats are also only found in Australia. They share a similar distribution as their tree-dwelling distant cousins, so they are mostly found in the southern and eastern states.

It's interesting to note that wombats are also found on the small southern island of Tasmania, although koalas are not, and there's no evidence that they ever lived there. This has led experts to believe that wombats must have been living in Tasmania *before* it separated from the mainland and became an island. While no koalas were anywhere near the region when it split.

UNIQUE CHARACTERISTICS AND APPEARANCE OF KOALAS

Koalas have evolved bodies to help them live comfortably on top of trees. They climb and latch onto the branches with their **strong limbs** and **sharp claws**. They have a superb sense of balance, so they don't fall off easily, and rough pads on their palms and soles that help them hold on tight. They also have strong cartilage (*soft tissue between joints*) on their butts, so they can comfortably balance on a tiny little tree branch.

The two **front paws** have five digits each, two of which are like our own thumbs and can be used to grip things like tree branches. On their **hind**

paws, koalas have two digits that are fused together – this creates what's known as a *'grooming claw,'* which they use for grooming themselves.

Koalas are also known for having lighter-colored fur on their chest, neck, chin, and inside their ears, with usually darker colors on their backs and legs. They may look a little chunky, but koalas are actually **muscular and lean**, with thick fur coverage that helps them deal with temperature extremes.

Another interesting aspect of a koala's body is its **pouch.** *Have you seen the pouch of a kangaroo?* For kangaroos, their pouch opens at the top, so their babies face upwards towards their heads. A koala's pouch faces downwards. **Don't worry, though, koalas have strong muscles to prevent joeys from falling out!**

Koalas have a very **slow metabolism**, which means they can take a long time to digest their food and have little energy left over. Naturally, this animal does a lot of sleeping!

Koalas retain their excellent sense of **smell and hearing** into adulthood. Their eyesight is quite poor, so they mostly rely on their ears and nose to get around and find their partner in mating season.

Speaking of which: *do you know how koalas search for a mate?* They scream for one at the very top of their voice!

Many people think koalas are placid and super quiet creatures, but in reality, they make a cacophony of **sounds**. Sound is how koalas mostly communicate with one another, of course! Koalas **grunt**, **bellow**, **snore**, and are even known to make blood-curdling **screams**, espe-cially when they are fighting one another for supremacy over a specific tree branch! These are seriously loud creatures!

Adult male koalas also have a very special **organ on their chest** that releases a sticky, smelly substance. Every koala has a unique scent, and to claim its home tree, a koala will rub this substance all over the tree's trunk. That's how it lets other koalas know that this tree is now taken!

Now here's something that is fascinating indeed: koalas have **the lowest brain-to-body-mass ratio**

in the animal world. This means that of all the animals of similar size, the koala has the smallest brain.

Does this make the koala a little...dumb?

Well, actually, yes! However, this is yet another clever trick of evolution.

The koala doesn't need to be a super-brainy Einstein. It eats, it sleeps, and it has no predator to worry about when it's up on a tree. The small brain capacity ensures that the little energy the koala gets from its food can be focused solely on keeping its body alive. *Doesn't that mean it is actually **THE smartest animal** of all?*

THE KOALA'S FAVORITE HABITAT

Koalas are happiest when they live in woodlands and open forests. However, since they have a limited diet, they are concentrated in areas where their favorite trees thrive in abundance. Given eucalyptus trees have a wide and scattered distribution in Australia, the koala population is likewise scattered. Mostly, however, they are found near water sources like lakes and rivers and all along the eastern coastline.

The diet of the koala is made up primarily of eucalyptus, although it will feed on other types of leaves if they happen to be conveniently close. However, a koala will never feed *solely* on non-eucalyptus trees. This makes reforestation for koala protection quite a tricky challenge.

To rehome a koala community in a new forest, the forest must be made up of *mostly* eucalyptus, alongside others. If that doesn't happen, the koalas will simply not thrive. Koalas spend most of their time in what's known as their '*home range*,' a small pocket of forest with several '*home trees*' – as the name suggests, these are trees that a koala chooses to be its primary home.

Koalas are very social animals and tend to live in large communities. Collectively, they need a lot of space to roam around.

All of these factors have created a dire situation for koala populations all over Australia. As their natural and wild forests are depleted or turned into farmlands, the habitat of the koalas is shrinking. Most koalas live in small pockets of protected forests, and many find themselves on privately owned land.

HOW MUCH DOES A KOALA EAT PER DAY?

Koalas can eat around two pounds of eucalyptus leaves per day. They actually get most of their daily water needs from the leaves and are not known to come to ground level in search of water very often. Only when their trees are empty of leaves does a koala actively search for a water source.

What is truly interesting is learning that eucalyptus leaves, despite their wonderful smell, are actually quite toxic. If we were to eat them, we would be poisoned and feel incredibly sick.

How come koalas don't get poisoned?

Because koalas have a neat superpower! The animal's digestive system releases a special enzyme that can break down and neutralize the toxins of eucalyptus trees, so the koala can get all the benefits minus the poisoning. *Pretty neat, right?*

What is *really* neat is the fact that this superpower is pretty rare, which means the koala does not compete for food with any other animals. Only other koalas! To be honest, this explains why the koala is such a slow and chill animal… it doesn't have to compete for food or hunt down prey. It only needs to find the right tree, and when it does, it can hang on to it for days and slowly eat its way around it.

This clever party trick is not something the koala is born with, mind you. The enzyme it needs to break down eucalyptus toxins is something that's passed on from mum to bub during the nursing-in-the-pouch period.

Eucalyptus leaves may contain a lot of water, but they lack serious nutrition. Koalas get very little energy from their diet, which is partly why they sleep so much and move around so little! Energy conservation, for this amazing animal, is key to its survival.

Out of the more than 700 distinct species of eucalyptus found in Australia, koalas only eat about 50.

FUN FACT: Koalas might have a restricted diet that consists mainly of eucalyptus leaves, but they are also very picky. They will go through a lot of effort to climb the highest tree branches to eat the sweetest and most tender leaves.

WHY DID THE KOALA EAT SO MUCH EUCALYPTUS?

He couldn't LEAF it alone!

THE LIFE CYCLE OF KOALAS

Mama koalas often only give birth to one baby each year, yet many females will only birth a young one every 3-4 years. Generally, in a 12-year lifespan, a female koala may give birth to about five to six joeys.

Koalas give birth after 35 days of pregnancy. At this stage, the joey is insanely tiny – only about half an inch long and merely 0.03 ounces in weight. *Imagine a pink jelly bean, if you will, one with no hair, no ears, and totally blind?* That's what a newborn koala joey looks like!

Within mere moments of being born, this koala-jelly-bean will use its well-developed sense of touch and smell to find its mama's pouch. It will crawl inside, attach to a nipple, and continue its **gestation** (*growth*) inside the pouch.

The next stage of a joey's growth is quite slow: the jelly bean will take about 5-6 months to fully develop its body, fur, eyes, and ears.

At this stage, the joey will begin to poke its curious head out of its mother's pouch to start investigating life on the 'outside.'

When the joey is about 7.5 months old, it will routinely pop out of the mum's pouch and spend time outside, riding on her back and eating her special droppings, called **pap**. This might sound gross, but it is actually very clever. You see, the mum's pap contains a lot of important enzymes that are crucial for the joey. They help the baby grow, and they also help its digestive system prepare for eating solid eucalyptus leaves.

After one full year, the joey is finally big and strong enough to permanently move out of mum's pouch. Young koalas will now have to find their own home and fend for themselves. Female koalas are usually ready to be mamas at around three to four years old. Usually, a joey will stay within its mother's home range up until the mum has another joey. After that, it will move out and find a new home range.

FUN FACT: Koalas may not be speed freaks, yet they are not nearly as slow as you might imagine. On the ground, a koala can stroll along at a very respectable speed of five miles an hour. *That's 30 times faster than a turtle or a sloth!*

HOW DO YOU KNOW WHEN A BABY KOALA BEAR IS HAPPY?

Because they jump for joey!

BONUS!
WHAT ARE OTHER ANIMALS THAT CAN ONLY BE FOUND IN AUSTRALIA?

Australia is home to a ton of unique animals found nowhere else on earth. If you are intrigued by koalas, we thought you might like to know what other unique animals this wonderful country has!

Kangaroos: The single most famous Australian animal and the national icon, the kangaroo, needs little introduction. *You know them, right?* They hop, they punch, kick, and scratch their bellies and are as cute as they come. As opposed to koalas, however, the kangaroo is faring well in Australia. In fact. The national animal outnumbers human inhabitants in the country two-to-one!

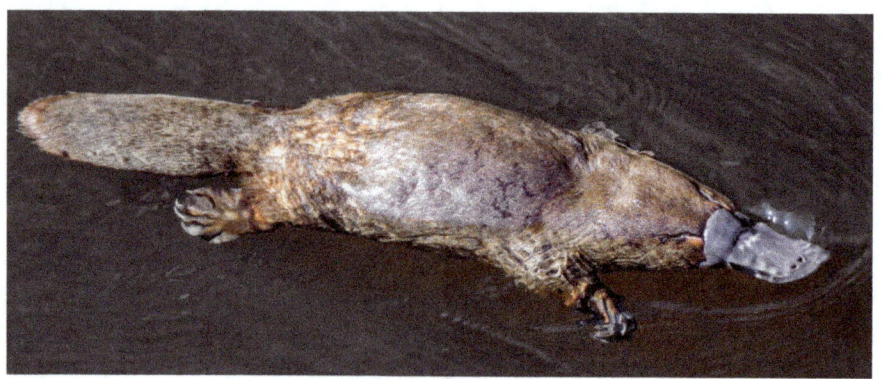

Platypus: A famous British biologist was once convinced that the platypus was a practical joke. He thought someone had sewn a duck's bill onto a beaver's body! Alas, not so. That's just what the bizarre and adorable platypus looks like! This incredibly unique animal is actually a mammal even though it lays eggs (*called a monotreme*).

Echidna: Together with the platypus, the Australian echidna is the only living monotreme left on earth. Adorable but spiky, this is *Down Under's* version of a porcupine!

Quokka: Known as the friendliest animal in Australia because they look like they are always smiling, quokkas are small kangaroo-like marsupials that only grow to about the size of a cat. They are rare and only found in a tiny little corner of Western Australia, and because they are unafraid of humans, they have become social media stars in the last decade or so!

Tasmanian devil: Bizarre enough to have been turned into a cartoon character by Looney Tunes decades ago, the Tassie devil is the largest **carnivorous** (meat-eating) marsupial in the world. This devil of a character emits one of the loudest and most disturbing screams in the animal world!

FIGHT FOR E-KOALA-TY!

HOW TO HELP THE KOALAS FROM AFAR!

We hope you enjoyed finding out all about the incredible koalas. If you'd love to help koalas thrive in the wild, share your love and knowledge with your friends and families so they too, can develop a passion for this fascinating animal.

If you live far away from Australia, there is still plenty that you can do to help protect this endangered wildlife species.

Adopt a koala: A small help goes a long way! Adopt a koala through Save the Koala (https://www.savethekoala.com/adopt-a-koala/) or gift an adoption to a dear friend who also loves them dearly. It would make a wonderful present for someone who cares!

Raise funds: Hold a fundraiser with your family or school class and donate funds to the Australian Koala Foundation.

Give a koala presentation: The more people know about the plight of koalas in Australia, the more help they can receive. Feel free to use this book to create a school presentation and share the koala love with your school friends and teachers!

Write a letter of support for the Koala Protection Act: Write a letter to the Australian Minister for Environment pledging your support of the Koala Protection Act. Make your voice loud and proud, and help koalas get the protection they deserve. You can ask an adult to help you draft a letter using this sample page - https://www.savethekoala.com/about-koalas/sample-letter/

THANK YOU!

Thank you for reading this book and for allowing us to share our love for koalas with you!

If you've enjoyed this book, please let us know by leaving a rating and a brief review wherever you made your purchase! This helps us spread the word to other readers!

Thank you for your time, and have an awesome day!

For more information, please visit:

www.animalreads.com

© Copyright 2023 - All rights reserved Admore Publishing

ISBN: 978-3-96772-140-9

ISBN: 978-3-96772-141-6

ISBN: 978-3-96772-142-3

Animal Reads at www.animalreads.com

The content contained within this book may not be reproduced, duplicated or transmitted without direct written permission from the author or the publisher.

Under no circumstances will any blame or legal responsibility be held against the publisher, or author, for any damages, reparation, or monetary loss due to the information contained within this book. Either directly or indirectly.

Published by Admore Publishing: Gotenstraße, Berlin, Germany

www.admorepublishing.com

www.ingramcontent.com/pod-product-compliance
Lightning Source LLC
LaVergne TN
LVHW020142080526
838202LV00048B/3990